THE ART OF NAPKIN FOLDING

THE ART OF
NAPKIN
FOLDING

BEAUTIFUL SHAPES FOR EVERY DINING OCCASION

Florence Sandeman

ARCTURUS

ARCTURUS

This edition published in 2014 by Arcturus Publishing Limited
26/27 Bickels Yard, 151–153 Bermondsey Street,
London SE1 3HA

Copyright © 2013 Arcturus Publishing Limited
Credits:
Cover image by Florence Sandeman; all other photography by Will
White, except for the photograph on page 7 (The Bridgeman Art
Library); illustrations by David Woodroffe

ISBN: 978-1-78212-638-6
AD001266UK

Printed in China

Contents

Introduction 6

Chapter 1
All about napkins 7

Chapter 2
Flat folds 14

Chapter 3
Standing folds................................... 32

Chapter 4
Napkins with objects........................... 52

Chapter 5
Picnic, buffet and party folds 64

Chapter 6
Novelty folds 78

Anthology of folds chart...................... 94

Index 96

Introduction

A well-laid table should be regarded as the beginning of any eating experience, from breakfast for one to a buffet for a hundred. While napkins are provided for functional purposes they can also be highly decorative, and choosing the right napkin and fold can greatly enhance the overall ambience of any dining occasion. Never was there a truer saying than 'you eat with your eyes'.

Plain white linen was once the standard form for napkins, but today we are spoilt for choice when it comes to the variety available. There is an ideal table setting and a perfect napkin for every occasion, whether it is a formal banquet or an informal family meal. This essential guide not only contains step-by-step instructions for more than 50 contemporary, traditional and novelty napkin folds, but also covers many other aspects of napkins including history, types, care and uses.

How to use this book

Of course the most obvious way to use the book is just to browse through from the beginning, but there are a couple of short cuts that may make finding the ideal napkin fold for a particular occasion much easier. At the back there is a general index, which lists napkin folds by name and type, such as flat folds, novelty folds, and folds suitable for parties, picnics and buffets.

On pages 94–95 you will also find a chart showing the attributes of all the folds contained in the book,

for example the most suitable size, the best material and how easy they are to make. This is a really useful chart to consult, especially if you do not have a range of napkins to choose from, as you can immediately exclude certain folds on the grounds of size, pattern or material.

The instructions for the individual folds are divided into chapters and are illustrated with photographs and line drawings, along with information such as suitability for particular occasions. However, please bear in mind that these are merely suggestions as to what type, size and pattern of napkin will work best. If you like a particular fold which suggests using medium-sized linen napkins, but you only have large paper napkins, it is worth giving it a go anyway.

Before you begin on the practical side of napkin folding, though, it is a good idea to read through the short preliminary chapter that covers napkin choices, placement and general place settings, which should make your experience of folding, using and choosing napkins both pleasurable and successful.

CHAPTER 1

All about napkins

While it is known that the Ancient Romans and Greeks used table linen, napkins as we would recognize them did not become commonplace in Europe until much later.

Central panel from the Altarpiece of the Holy Sacrament (1464–68) by Dirck Bouts. This depiction of the Last Supper illustrates swagged fabric, which was used as a form of napkin.

By the 12th century, table settings consisted of a large central cloth with a separate outer border, which often draped over the edges and down the sides of the table. Cutlery, in particular individual forks, was not widely used until the 1800s; until that time, diners relied on their hands to transport food to their mouths. Larger pieces of food such as joints of meat would make a mess of diners' mouths and faces too, and it was common for everyone to wipe their hands and faces on the swagged fabric, using it as a form of napkin. These separate borders would need to be changed several times during a banquet.

Above: *Early on, table linens were not thought of as decorative. Most table linens were naturally coloured or white as they were made from hemp or linen.*

Individual napkins were first used in the French royal court around 1400, having originated in the city of Reims, France, known for its fine cloth. The city even presented King Charles VII with a set of table napkins to mark his coronation in 1429. Dining customs and etiquette were in the main set by the Italian and French courts, but their practices quickly spread to northern Europe and Britain.

The advent of utensils for eating made dining an altogether more refined affair, and hosts began to provide individual napkins for their guests. The use of tablecloths and napkins rapidly spread from the

Left: *An example of a 15th-century table setting with individual napkins placed for each diner.*
Below: *Illustrations of napkin folding, published in 1657.*

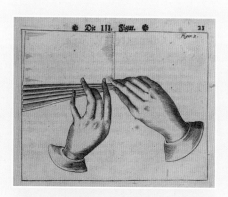
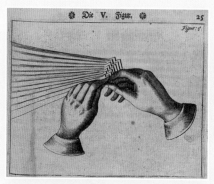
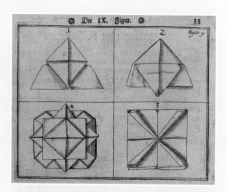
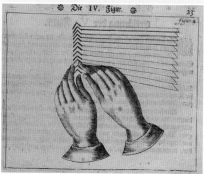
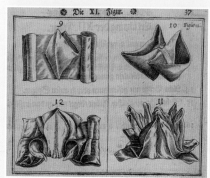
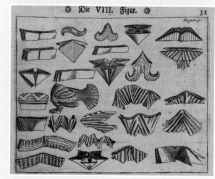

aristocracy to the merchant classes, and by the 15th century, even less affluent households would own at least one tablecloth plus individual cloths which probably doubled as wrapping for various items connected with dining. The size of individual napkins changed a good deal through the ages, ranging from small cloths akin to our cocktail napkins to very large ones, according to fashion and practicalities; during Elizabethan times, for example, when ruffs became a popular and expensive item of clothing, napkins generous enough to tie around the neck were required to protect them.

Above: *By the 16th-century, napkins were an accepted refinement of dining, a cloth made in different sizes for various events.*

Surprisingly, once the dining fork became widely used by European royalty in the 17th century the napkin fell out of favour among the upper classes, with the emphasis being placed more on neatness when eating, reinforced with an abundance of new rules for dining etiquette. When napkins made a reappearance in the 1770s, etiquette was developed on how and when to use them, making them much more a feature of the table. By the late 1800s, decorative ways of folding them to enhance the look of the place settings had become a fashion that still prevails today.

Above and below: *Decorative napkin folds enhance the look of formal table settings.*

Choosing and caring for your napkins

The range of napkins now is a vast and potentially bewildering one, but what matters most is to choose ones that you like. With the aid of this book, you will be able to find many folds that are suitable for any napkin. Here are a few additional tips to guide you.

- All the folds in this book are shown with square napkins, so to make life easy, buy square ones. However, be aware that some vintage napkins may be oblong or slightly off-square.

- If you want to use patterned napkins, choosing ones that are patterned on both sides is advisable as it ensures that completed folds will look correct.

- If you are limited as to the number of napkins you can buy, go for plain white (or a colour that goes well with your crockery) in fabrics such as cotton or linen that will hold a crease, rather than unusual patterns or synthetic materials.

- Pay attention to the size: medium-sized napkins can be folded to suit most occasions, whereas small or large ones can look very out of place in certain circumstances.

- Paper napkins have their place and should not be dismissed out of hand. Having a stock of medium or large paper serviettes will come in very handy, especially for less formal occasions such as morning coffee, afternoon tea or sun-downers with nibbles where a less substantial napkin is all that is required.

- If finances are restricted, second-hand napkins are usually most acceptable. For most of us, napkins are not used on a daily basis so even a vintage napkin can be in very good condition. Charity shops are a good place to source second-hand items at very reasonable prices.

- Do not be afraid to mix and match napkins. There is no rule that all napkins on a table should be exactly the same.

- If you get the opportunity to purchase coordinated items such as tablecloths, place mats or napkin rings, seize it as you may not be so lucky again.

Care

Brand-new napkins should be laundered before use to rid them of any manufacturing residues which may remain on the fabric, and all napkins should be laundered after each use. A biological detergent may be necessary, especially if there are lipstick stains. If you handwash your napkins, make sure that they are well rinsed before they are dried.

If you want to save time, buying soluble starch to put in the rinse cycle of your washing machine is an option. However, it is easy to apply spray starch when you are ironing newly laundered napkins or just before folding.

Unless you know you will be using your napkins every week or so, it is a good idea to wrap them, washed and ironed, in paper, fabric or even in a pillowcase before storing in a cupboard. It is surprising how draughts can make dust particles collect along ridges, leaving unsightly dark lines.

Practicalities

While napkin folding allows plenty of room for choice and creativity, as a general rule, use smaller napkins for light meals and large ones for dinner or substantial lunches. There is no point in supplying large dinner napkins at cocktail parties when all that is required is a piece of fabric or paper on which to wipe fingertips that have picked up crisps or crostini.

Allow the particular occasion to dictate the type and style of napkin you use. Boldly patterned napkins are best for informal occasions, while small, dainty lace napkins are ideal for afternoon tea; paper napkins are most suitable for large, informal gatherings such as picnics, barbecues or parties where people move around with their food and drink and are likely to put their napkin down somewhere, never to be seen again.

Napkin sizes

A beverage napkin, used when serving drinks and hors d'oeuvres, is square, like most cloth napkins, and about 12.5cm/5in to each side. A luncheon napkin is 5cm/2in larger, and a dinner napkin larger still. As a guide, small napkins measure up to 30cm/12in square, medium napkins are 32–44cm/13–17in and large napkins are 45cm/18in or more. It may be difficult to find napkins larger than 45cm/18in in stores, but you will be able to source them online.

Placement

The placement of napkins is not important except on formal occasions, when they should be positioned to the left of the place setting, either on the side plate or directly on the table top. They can also be placed directly in front of the diner, on a charger plate if one is being used, or between the knives on the right and the forks on the left. Never put the napkin directly on the diner's chair; even on very formal occasions, when the table may be full of crockery, cutlery and flower arrangements, find room for the napkin. The Tall Candle fold in this book (see p.82) only takes up the smallest amount of space on the table, using the largest of napkins.

General tips for creating perfect folds

There are a few practical tips that will make napkin folding easier, whether you are a novice or not.

- Clear ample space on a table or ironing board so you are not inhibited by cramped conditions.

- Have any props such as napkin rings ready to hand before starting the fold.

- Iron all creases out of the napkins before starting to fold, spraying with starch if necessary.

- Many of the more complicated folds benefit from being ironed throughout the steps, so having a hot iron to hand is a good plan of action.

- You might want to practise the fold several times on one of the napkins which you will be using. This is especially useful for some of the more complex folds and for mastering precision accordion pleats and folds.

Flat and horizontal These are folds that lie relatively flat on the surface. It is their nature to take up more space than other types of folds.

Standing As the name implies, these folds stand upright and can give contour to your table settings.

Objects These folds utilize objects such as glasses or gifts as an intrinsic part of the design.

Types of folds

The following pages contain more than 50 folds which have been divided into the following sections.

Picnics, buffets and parties Most of the napkins in this category are suitable for holding individual place settings, many of which can be prepared in advance and transported to another location such as a picnic.

Novelty These tend to be more complex folds in the shape of objects such as a rabbit or rose. Many are perfect for children's gatherings or special occasions such as Valentine's Day.

13

CHAPTER 2

Flat folds

Some of the easiest folds are to be found in this first section. However, don't let that mislead you into thinking they will be uninspiring or only for informal occasions.

Here you will find folds for most settings, from compact designs such as the Summer Bud which are suitable for a simple breakfast or luncheon tray to more complex folds such as the Water Lily, which could grace any formal dinner setting. What they all have in common is that they lie relatively flat and are therefore suitable for placing on side plates, cover plates or chargers, or directly on the table.

As some of these folds are quite wide, it is a good idea to use plainer napkins to avoid an over-busy look to the finished table. If space is limited, a few of the folds – for example the Spearhead and Spring Roll – can be made more compact just by using smaller napkins, although you will probably need to spend a little more time preparing them.

Many folds in this group are excellent for paper napkins, as they don't need so much body as folds which need to be stood up or folded in many steps.

Summer Bud

This is a compact little design which is quick and easy to fold, ideal for an informal setting. It is one of the few folds that looks better when smaller napkins or paper serviettes are used. To create a summery feel, use pastel paper or fabric napkins with a small flowery print.

1 Place the napkin reverse side up, one corner towards you. Fold in half horizontally from bottom to top to form a triangle with the open ends facing away from you.

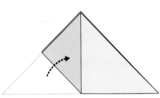

2 Fold the left-hand corner upwards to meet the tip of the triangle so that the bottom edge falls along the centre line.

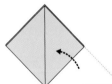

3 Fold the right-hand corner upwards in the same way so that the two bottom edges meet in the centre.

4 Turn the napkin over so that the open ends are still facing away from you in a diamond shape.

5 Fold the diamond in half horizontally from bottom to top, creating a triangle.

6 Turn the napkin over, then fold the right-hand and left-hand points over towards the centre. Tuck one side into the folds of the other to secure.

7 Turn the napkin over again, gently open up the centre and place it on a plate, either flat or standing upright.

EASE	NAPKIN SIZE	SUITABLE MATERIALS	NAPKIN DESIGN	STARCHED
Easy	Small – Medium	Any	Plain – Patterned	Optional

Clutch Bag

This fold is easy, quick and can be made with any fabric that will hold a crease. Use plain starched close-weave fabrics for formal settings or patterned, unstarched or open-weave napkins for a softer look on informal occasions. It is suitable for contemporary settings.

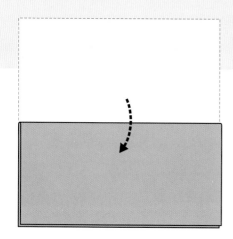

1 Place the napkin reverse side up, then fold in half horizontally from top to bottom so that the open ends are nearest to you.

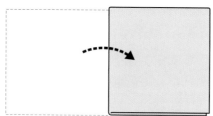

2 Fold in half vertically from left to right to form a square with the open ends facing the right and bottom.

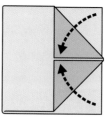

3 Fold the top and bottom right corners of the top two layers of the square so that they meet at the centre and form a point facing to the right.

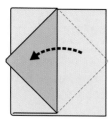

4 Fold the top two layers to the left vertically along the centre line so that the point projects slightly over the left-hand edge of the square.

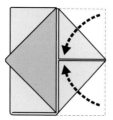

5 Fold the top and bottom right corners of the remaining two layers of the square so that they meet at the centre and form a point facing to the right.

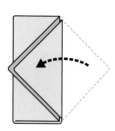

6 Fold the point over to the left so it lies on top of the first point but slightly offset, making sure that the slanted edges and points are parallel and even.

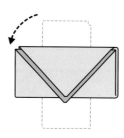

7 Rotate the napkin so that the long edges are at the top and bottom with the points facing downwards.

EASE	NAPKIN SIZE	SUITABLE MATERIALS	NAPKIN DESIGN	STARCHED
Easy	Any	Any	Any	Optional

Tri Pleat

Although this fold is made up of only three steps and is classed as easy, some adjustments may be required to get the pleats even. It is an excellent fold for small napkins. Starched napkins will produce a crisper finish, though starching is not strictly necessary so long as the material can hold a crease.

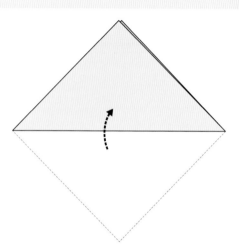

1 Place the napkin reverse side up, one corner towards you, then fold in half from bottom to top to create a triangle.

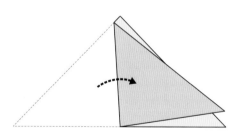

2 Fold the left-hand corner of the triangle across to the right at the centre point, so that you have two points on the right.

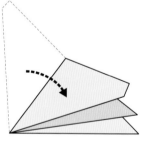

3 Fold the left edge to the right from the bottom centre so that the third and final pleat is parallel and the same width as the previous pleats.

EASE	NAPKIN SIZE	SUITABLE MATERIALS	NAPKIN DESIGN	STARCHED
Easy	Small – Medium	Linen – Cotton – Synthetic mixed – Paper	Plain – Decorated	Optional

Water Lily

Using napkins which are absolutely square and starched helps to create the perfect result more easily. A bread roll or gift can be placed in the centre of the finished fold, which will keep it flat and in shape once placed on the table.

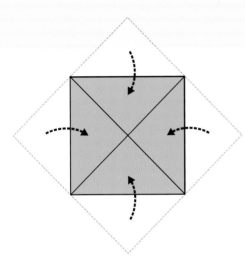

1 Lay the napkin reverse side up, then fold all four corners diagonally so that they touch in the centre, forming a smaller square.

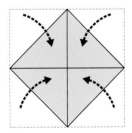

2 Fold the four new corners of the napkin to the centre of the smaller square.

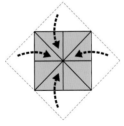

3 Turn the napkin over and fold all four corners so that they touch in the centre as before.

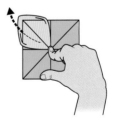

4 Holding the centre points down with your fingers, reach underneath each outer point and pull the flaps under each corner upwards and inwards so that they form a cupped edge.

EASE	NAPKIN SIZE	SUITABLE MATERIALS	NAPKIN DESIGN	STARCHED
Intermediate	Medium – Large	Linen – Cotton – Synthetics	Plain	Yes

Humetty Cross

Although this fold consists of many steps, once the basics have been mastered it can be folded more quickly than you might expect. It is one of the few more complicated folds which can be done with a small napkin. Choose close-weaved fabrics which hold a crease, or use paper. Starching is highly recommended, and ironing after each step makes the folding easier.

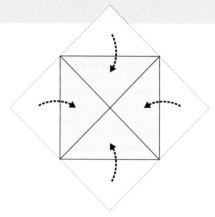

1 Lay the napkin reverse side up, then fold all four corners diagonally so that they meet at the centre.

2 Carefully turn the napkin over. Ironing all the creases first will help to keep the folds in place.

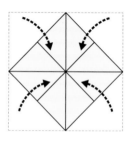

3 Fold all four corners to the centre diagonally so that the points touch at the centre as you did in Step 1. Press with an iron again if necessary to keep all the folds flat and in place.

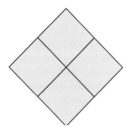

4 Carefully turn the napkin over again.

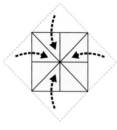

5 Repeat Step 3, folding all four corners diagonally so that the points meet in the centre.

6 Turn the napkin over and press well.

7 Lift one of the centre points and pull its two edges apart, which will make it open up and flatten into a small rectangle shape.

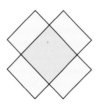

8 Repeat with the other three centre points and then press firmly.

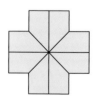

9 Turn the napkin over and press again so that it lies very flat.

EASE	NAPKIN SIZE	SUITABLE MATERIALS	NAPKIN DESIGN	STARCHED
Difficult	Any	Fine linen – Cotton – Paper	Any	Yes

Iced Diamond

This geometric design is a cross between an ice cream cornet and a faceted diamond. Use smooth, plain, starched napkins in a modern setting for the best effect.

1 Place the napkin reverse side up, then fold in half from bottom to top so that the open ends are facing away from you.

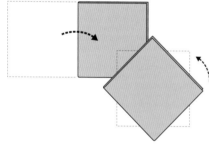

2 Fold in half vertically from left to right to make a square, then rotate it so it forms a diamond with the open ends facing away from you.

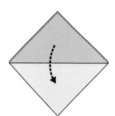

3 Fold the top corners of the top two layers in half horizontally.

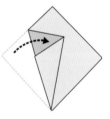

4 Turn the napkin over, then fold the left-hand side over about one-third towards the right.

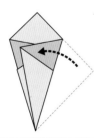

5 Fold the right-hand side towards the left in the same way so that the edge echoes the angle of the left-hand edge and the napkin forms a long, symmetrical diamond shape.

6 Tuck the top corner of the right-hand flap behind the fold underneath to secure it.

EASE	NAPKIN SIZE	SUITABLE MATERIALS	NAPKIN DESIGN	STARCHED
Intermediate	Small – Medium	Linen – Cotton – Synthetic blends – Paper	Plain	Yes

Kimono

Once you have mastered making narrow, even pleats, this fold can be achieved relatively quickly and would add an appropriate finishing touch when serving oriental-themed meals. A starched napkin makes the precision folding of the pleats easier, as does having an iron available both during and at the end of folding. This napkin can also be used as a base on which to rest chopsticks.

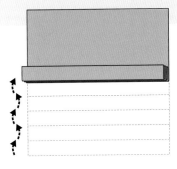

1 Place the napkin right side up, then, starting at the bottom, accordion pleat the bottom of the napkin like a fan, stopping halfway up.

2 Turn the napkin over so that the pleats are lying horizontally underneath the top edge.

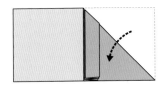

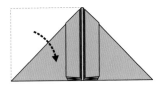

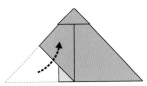

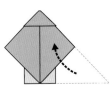

3 Fold the top right-hand corner downwards at a 45-degree angle so that the top edge of the pleats is lying along the centre of the napkin and the corner is touching the bottom line.

4 Repeat with the left-hand corner so that the top edges of the pleats meet in the centre and the overall shape is a triangle.

5 Turn the napkin over from side to side, with the long edge of the triangle remaining at the bottom. Fold the left-hand bottom corner upwards and tuck it into the little pocket at the top of the triangle.

6 Repeat Step 5 with the right-hand corner.

7 Turn the napkin over from side to side so that the open pleats are at the bottom.

EASE	NAPKIN SIZE	SUITABLE MATERIALS	NAPKIN DESIGN	STARCHED
Intermediate	Medium – Large	Linen – Cotton – Paper	Plain – Self-patterned	Yes

23

The Mortar Board

This is an elegant fold, reminiscent of graduates' hats, which works well in contemporary settings. The napkins can be folded and stacked in good time before they are needed. Even without starching or ironing the creases, this fold looks smart.

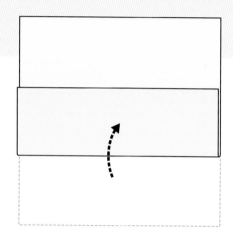

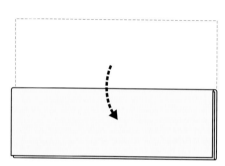

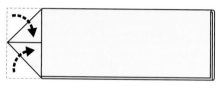

1 Place the napkin reverse side up and fold the bottom third upwards.

2 Fold the top third downwards to create a wide rectangle.

3 Fold the two left-hand corners across so that they meet in the middle, forming two little triangles and a point at the left-hand edge.

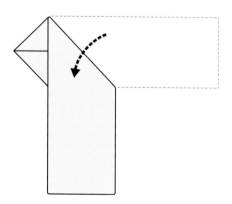

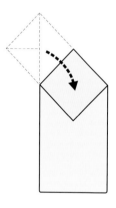

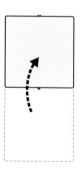

4 Fold the right-hand portion downwards so that the top edge meets the edges of the two little triangles.

5 Fold the top corner downwards at a 45-degree angle so that the top corner meets the right-hand corner.

6 Turn the napkin over with the pointed end away from you, then fold in half upwards. Turn the napkin over again.

EASE	NAPKIN SIZE	SUITABLE MATERIALS	NAPKIN DESIGN	STARCHED
Intermediate	Medium – Large	Linen – Cotton – Paper	Plain	Optional

Palm Leaf

This fold is easy, quick and suitable for fabric or paper napkins. Use plain starched napkins for formal settings, as making the pleats narrower will create a crisper, formal look. Care needs to be taken when choosing the napkin ring, especially for small napkins, when it may be better to use ribbon or other types of small fabric or elastic rings.

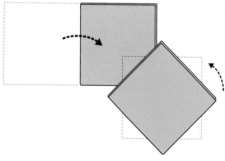

1 Place the napkin reverse side up, then fold in half from bottom to top so that the open ends are facing away from you.

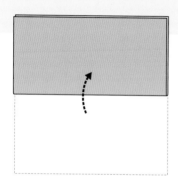

2 Fold the napkin in half vertically, then arrange it in a diamond shape with the open ends facing away from you.

3 With a napkin ring to hand, make 4–6 small vertical pleats about a quarter of the way down from the top.

4 Slip the top quarter of the napkin into the napkin ring.

EASE	NAPKIN SIZE	SUITABLE MATERIALS	NAPKIN DESIGN	STARCHED
Easy	Small – Medium	Any	Plain – Patterned	Yes

Purity Square

This pretty fold is perfect for lace-trimmed, scallop-edged napkins or those with corner designs. Use a starched white cotton napkin with corner embroidery or cut-out motif to emphasize the theme.

1 Place the napkin reverse side up with one corner pointing towards you – if you are using a napkin with a single corner decoration, place this at the top corner. Fold in half horizontally from bottom to top to form a triangle with the fold nearest to you.

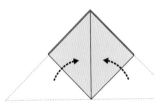

2 Fold the left-hand and right-hand corners upwards to meet the tip of the triangle so that the bottom edges meet along the centre line, forming a diamond shape.

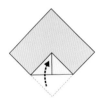

3 Turn the napkin over from side to side so that the open ends are still facing away from you in a diamond shape, then turn the bottom point up so it just touches the centre of the diamond.

4 Turn the napkin over again then fold the left and right sides over so that the bottom edges meet and lie along the centre vertical line, forming another overall diamond.

5 Turn the napkin over from side to side so that the open ends are facing away from you.

6 Lift the top corner of the nearest little square which has been formed then gently pull the two edges apart and flatten into a rectangle.

7 Lay the napkin flat on the table or on a plate.

EASE	NAPKIN SIZE	SUITABLE MATERIALS	NAPKIN DESIGN	STARCHED
Intermediate	Small – Medium	Linen – Cotton – Paper	Plain – Decorated	Yes

Spearhead

For this fold you will need to use napkins that are square to ensure the chevrons line up accurately. Using an iron throughout makes for a crisper finish and helps the napkin to lie flatter. Plain, well-starched napkins are most suitable for this fold.

1 Place the napkin reverse side up, then fold in half from bottom to top so that the open ends are facing away from you.

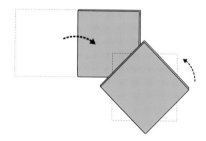

2 Fold in half vertically to make a square, then rotate the napkin so it forms a diamond with the open ends facing away from you.

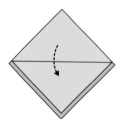

3 Fold down the top layer almost in half, leaving a small border at the lower edges. Make sure the borders and edges are even and parallel with the bottom part and press down firmly along the fold.

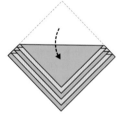

4 Fold the remaining layers downwards in the same way, once again leaving small borders and making sure the borders and edges are all even and lie parallel with each other. Press firmly along all the creases.

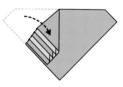

5 Turn the napkin over from side to side, then fold the left-hand point downwards so that the top edge lies along the vertical line.

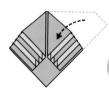

6 Repeat with the right-hand side, making sure that the top edges just meet along the vertical line. Press well.

EASE	NAPKIN SIZE	SUITABLE MATERIALS	NAPKIN DESIGN	STARCHED
Intermediate	Small – Medium	Linen – Cotton – Paper	Plain – Bordered	Yes

Spring Roll

Relatively easy to achieve, this fold is suitable for soft, unstarched, open-weave fabrics. Even with a large napkin, it creates a compact design which fits easily on a small side plate. It is an excellent choice for any meal which can be eaten with chopsticks.

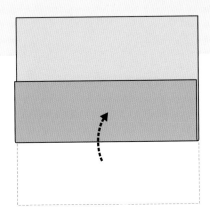

1 Place the napkin reverse side up and fold the bottom third upwards.

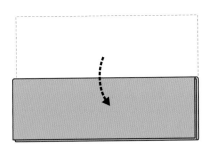

2 Fold the top third downwards to create a wide rectangle.

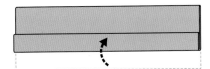

3 Fold the bottom up almost to the middle and press firmly along the fold.

4 Turn the napkin over, positioning it to form a long vertical rectangle.

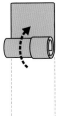

5 Starting from the short end nearest to you, roll up relatively tightly. Place on the table or on a plate, seam side down to prevent it unrolling.

EASE	NAPKIN SIZE	SUITABLE MATERIALS	NAPKIN DESIGN	STARCHED
Easy	Medium – Large	Linen – Thick cotton	Plain – Bordered – Patterned	No

Steps

Using plain napkins accentuates the three-dimensional nature of this lovely architectural fold. Take care to make the 'steps' even and parallel. Starching the napkin and ironing after each step will help create a perfect end result.

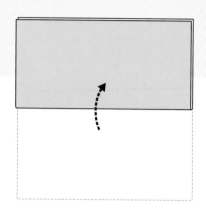

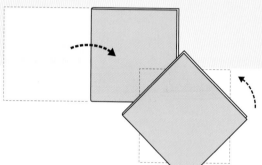

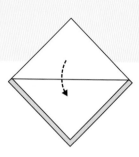

1 Lay the napkin reverse side up then fold in half from bottom to top so that the open ends are facing away from you.

2 Fold in half vertically to form a square then turn the napkin so it forms a diamond with the open ends facing away from you.

3 Fold down the top layer from just above the centre, leaving a small border at the lower edges. Make sure that the borders and edges are even and parallel with the bottom part and press down firmly along the fold.

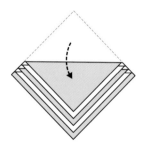

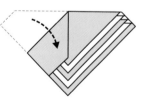

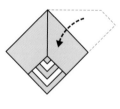

4 Fold the remaining layers downwards in the same way, again leaving small borders and making sure the borders and edges are all even and lie parallel with each other. Press firmly along all creases.

5 Fold the left-hand corner downwards at a 45-degree angle so that the top edge lies along the centre vertical line.

6 Repeat with the right-hand side, creating an overall diamond shape.

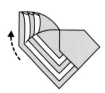

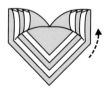

7 Fold the top point over to the back by about a quarter.

8 Fold the top left-hand layers upwards and away from you to create the 'steps'.

9 Repeat with the right-hand side.

EASE	NAPKIN SIZE	SUITABLE MATERIALS	NAPKIN DESIGN	STARCHED
Intermediate	Medium	Linen – Cotton – Paper	Plain – Bordered	Yes

CHAPTER 3

Standing folds

As the name implies, these folds stand up and therefore add height and dimension to table settings. Many of them have the added bonus of taking up less table space than horizontal folds, making them perfect for more formal settings where the table may be laid with extra crockery, cutlery, glassware or other objects such as candle sticks or flower arrangements.

This group contains many old favourites, including the Bishop's Mitre and Lady Windermere's Fan, both of which were restaurant staples, and the gorgeous Bird of Paradise, sometimes known as the Cockscomb. There are also modern folds such as the Catamaran as well as really easy folds – for example the Marquee, which can be completed in less than a minute.

In general, the larger the napkin used, the taller the end result will be. Certain folds will not work well with very large or unstarched napkins, so be guided by the notes at the beginning and end of each fold until you are more practised in the art of napkin folding.

Pyramid

Quick and easy to achieve, this fold is a good choice for large gatherings, especially as the napkins can be folded in advance and stacked until needed. Use starched close-weave materials such as cotton or linen to ensure that the end fold stands up correctly.

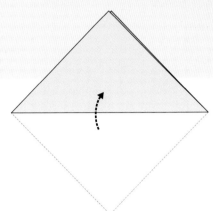

1 Place the napkin reverse side up, one corner towards you. Fold the bottom corner up to meet the top, forming a triangle with the fold nearest to you.

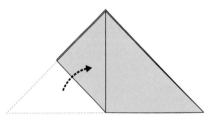

2 Fold the left-hand corner upwards to meet the tip of the triangle so the bottom falls along the centre line.

3 Fold the right-hand corner upwards in the same way so that the two bottom edges meet in the centre.

4 Turn the napkin over so that the open ends are still facing away from you in a diamond shape.

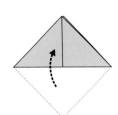

5 Fold the diamond in half upwards, creating a triangle. Turn the napkin over from side to side, keeping the point of the triangle at the top.

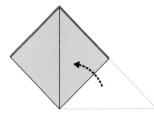

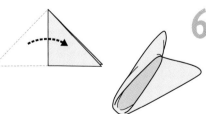

6 Fold the triangle in half from left to right along the centre line, then stand the napkin upright on the longest edge and spread the points out a little to stabilize it.

EASE	NAPKIN SIZE	SUITABLE MATERIALS	NAPKIN DESIGN	STARCHED
Easy	Small – Medium	Linen – Cotton – Synthetics	Plain – Patterned	Yes

Atrium Lily

Some of the steps here cannot be accurately described, so this fold can be a little tricky – you will need to rely on your own visual judgment to ensure symmetry. Using starched close-weave materials such as cotton makes the fold easier to achieve, as does ironing the folds once they are made.

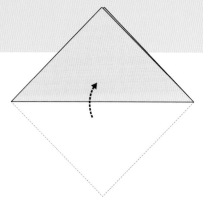

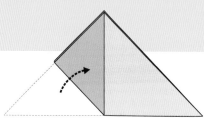

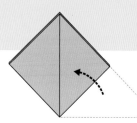

1 Place the napkin reverse side up with one corner towards you. Fold in half from bottom to top to form a triangle with the fold nearest to you.

2 Fold the left-hand corner upwards to meet the tip of the triangle so that the bottom edge falls along the centre vertical line.

3 Fold the right-hand corner upwards in the same way so that the two bottom edges meet in the centre to form a diamond shape.

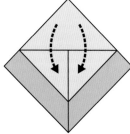

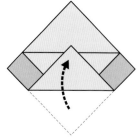

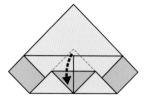

4 Fold the top left-hand and right-hand points down by about three-quarters so that the fold is just above the halfway line of the overall diamond shape.

5 Fold the bottom point of the overall diamond up to the centre of the diamond.

6 Fold the point back over itself so that the tip just touches the bottom edge.

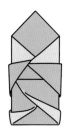

7 Turn the napkin over from side to side then fold the right and left points over towards the centre and tuck one side into the folds of the other to secure, making sure both sides are symmetrical.

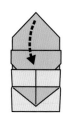

8 Fold the point of the top layer point towards you, tucking it behind the fold below, then stand the napkin upright.

EASE	NAPKIN SIZE	SUITABLE MATERIALS	NAPKIN DESIGN	STARCHED
Difficult	Medium – Large	Linen – Cotton – Synthetics	Plain – Self-patterned	Yes

Marquee

The Marquee fold can be used to stunning effect for larger dining occasions such as weddings or banquets as well as intimate gatherings. Provided your napkin is absolutely square, even small cocktail napkins can be used, as well as those with a decorative edge or corner motif.

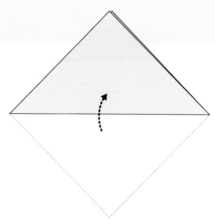

1 Place the napkin reverse side up, one corner towards you. Fold the bottom corner to meet the top, forming a triangle with the fold nearest to you.

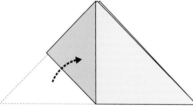

2 Fold the left-hand corner upwards to meet the tip of the triangle so the bottom falls along the centre line.

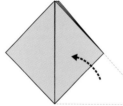

3 Fold the right-hand corner upwards in the same way so that the two bottom edges meet in the centre.

4 Turn the napkin over so the open ends are still facing away from you in a diamond shape.

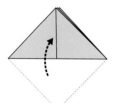

5 Fold the diamond in half upwards, creating a triangle.

6 Fold the triangle in half from right to left along the centre line.

7 Stand the napkin upright and spread the points out a little to stabilize it.

EASE	NAPKIN SIZE	SUITABLE MATERIALS	NAPKIN DESIGN	STARCHED
Easy	*Any*	*Linen – Thick cotton*	*Plain – Bordered – Corner motif*	*Yes*

The Crown

This is another relatively easy fold to achieve, provided starched napkins are used and a little care is taken to make sure the end design is symmetrical. Although small and large napkins can be used, medium ones create the best end result – neither too tall nor too short.

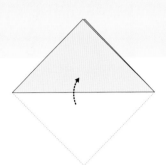

1 Place the napkin reverse side up with one corner pointing towards you. Fold in half from bottom to top to form a triangle with the fold nearest to you.

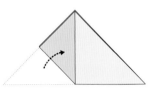

2 Fold the left-hand corner upwards to meet the tip of the triangle so the bottom edge falls along the centre line.

3 Fold the right-hand corner upwards in the same way, with the two bottom edges meeting in the centre.

4 Turn the napkin over from side to side, keeping the open ends furthest away from you. Fold in half from bottom to top, creating a triangle with the fold nearest to you.

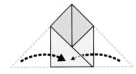

5 Fold the right-hand and left-hand corners over towards the middle, tucking one side into the folds of the other side to secure.

6 Stand the napkin upright, arranging the two loose flaps to arch over to each side.

EASE	NAPKIN SIZE	SUITABLE MATERIALS	NAPKIN DESIGN	STARCHED
Intermediate	Any	Linen – Cotton – Paper	Plain – Self-patterned	Yes

Waterfall

For this fold, use close-weave napkins such as fine linen or cotton which have been well starched. Ironing the pleats as soon as you've finished Step 3 will make handling the napkin easier without the pleats falling out and also makes for a crisper finish. Plain napkins look best.

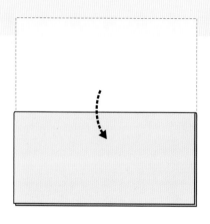

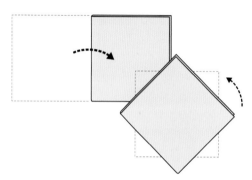

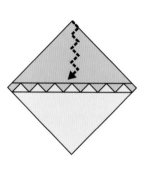

1 Place the napkin reverse side up, then fold in half from top to bottom so the open ends are nearest to you.

2 Fold in half vertically to make a square, then rotate it to a diamond with the open ends facing away from you.

3 Make horizontal accordion pleats in the top layer only (there should be four layers), starting at the top point and stopping when you get halfway down the diamond. Make the pleats as narrow and even as you can and press them down using an iron.

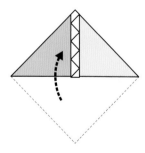

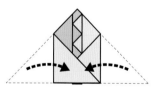

4 Very carefully, turn the napkin over from side to side, making sure the pleats stay in place. Fold the napkin in half vertically, then rotate it so that it forms a triangle with the fold nearest to you.

5 Fold the left-hand and right-hand points towards the centre, tucking one side into the folds of the other to secure it. Make sure you keep the symmetry of the top point.

6 Stand the napkin up so that the pleats fall open to form the waterfall.

EASE	NAPKIN SIZE	SUITABLE MATERIALS	NAPKIN DESIGN	STARCHED
Intermediate	Any	Linen – Cotton – Paper	Plain	Yes

Bird of Paradise

This beautiful fold can be tricky, especially if thicker materials or smaller napkins are used. Accurate folding and patience are needed to create it, but the end result is well worth the effort.

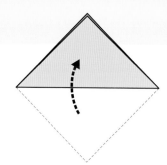

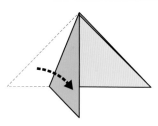

1 Place the napkin reverse side up. Fold it in half horizontally, then in half again vertically to form a square with the open ends at the top and right-hand side.

2 Rotate the napkin so it forms a diamond shape with the open corners facing you, then fold in half horizontally from bottom to top to form a triangle with all the single layers on top and the open ends facing away from you.

3 Making sure all the single layers are on top (there should be four), fold the left-hand point of the triangle downwards so that the left-hand edge lies vertically along the centre line.

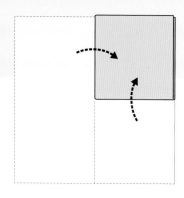

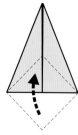

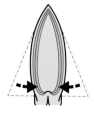

4 Repeat with the right-hand side so that the edges meet along the centre line.

5 Fold the two points at the bottom underneath so the bottom edge is straight, creating a tall triangle.

6 Fold the triangle in half vertically so that the two points you just turned under are on the inside and all the pointed layers are visible.

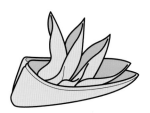

7 Pull up the top single layer at the point until it stands upright.

8 Repeat with the next three layers, spacing them equally apart, then stand the finished fold upright.

EASE	NAPKIN SIZE	SUITABLE MATERIALS	NAPKIN DESIGN	STARCHED
Difficult	Large	Linen – Cotton – Paper	Plain	Yes

Bishop's Mitre

A classic fold, this was popularized by its use in restaurants, where a dinner roll was often placed in the cavity of the fold. A starched napkin is essential to ensure the end fold looks crisp, stands upright and stays in shape. Plain napkins tend to look better. Although white is the usual choice for traditional settings, do not be afraid to choose a colour that complements the rest of your table setting.

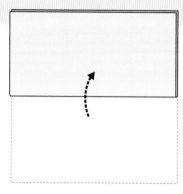

1 Place the napkin reverse side up, then fold in half horizontally from bottom to top so that the fold is nearest to you.

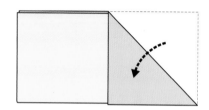

2 Fold the top right-hand corners downwards so that the corner is touching the bottom edge in the centre.

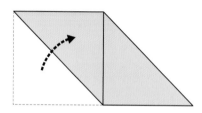

3 Fold the bottom left-hand corner upwards, with the corner touching the top edge in the centre and meeting the right-hand flap along the centre line.

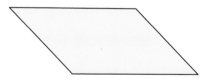

4 Turn the napkin over and rotate it so that the long folded edges are horizontal.

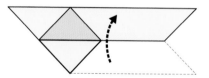

5 Fold the napkin horizontally in half from bottom to top. A small triangular piece of napkin will be left behind on the left-hand side.

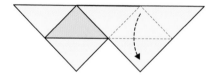

6 Reach underneath the right-hand side of the napkin and pull out the triangular flap which corresponds with the left-hand side, forming two small triangles.

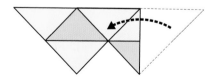

7 Fold the right triangle in half vertically along its centre line.

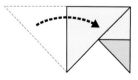

8 Fold the extreme left-hand corner over to the right, tucking it into the folds of the right-hand flap you just folded over to secure. Press all the folds well.

9 Pull apart the two straight edges then stand the fold upright with the points facing upwards. There will be a hole in the centre.

EASE	NAPKIN SIZE	SUITABLE MATERIALS	NAPKIN DESIGN	STARCHED
Intermediate	Any	Linen – Cotton mixes – Paper	Plain	Yes

Cardinal's Hat

This design is quick and simple to fold. The larger the napkin, the taller the hat. Starched close-weave materials such as cotton look best and make the fold easier to achieve.

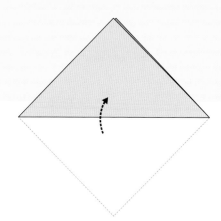

1 Place the napkin reverse side up with one corner pointing towards you. Fold in half from bottom to top to form a triangle with the fold nearest to you.

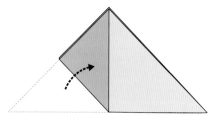

2 Fold the left-hand corner upwards to meet the tip of the triangle so that the bottom edge falls along the centre line.

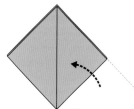

3 Fold the right-hand corner upwards in the same way, with the two bottom edges meeting in the centre.

4 Turn the napkin over from side to side so that the open ends are still facing away from you in a diamond shape.

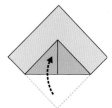

5 Fold the bottom third of the diamond upwards.

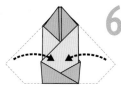

6 Turn the napkin over from side to side. Fold the right and left points about a third of the way over towards the centre and tuck one side into the folds of the other side to secure, making sure both sides are symmetrical and the point is in the centre.

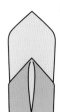

7 Stand upright with the point upwards.

EASE	NAPKIN SIZE	SUITABLE MATERIALS	NAPKIN DESIGN	STARCHED
Easy	Any	Linen – Cotton – Paper	Plain	Yes

Catamaran

Relatively easy, this fold is ideal for informal dining. Use starched close-weave napkins to ensure they stand upright. Plain napkins look best.

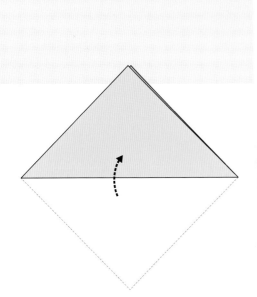

1 Place the napkin reverse side up, one corner towards you, then fold in half from bottom to top to form a triangle with the open ends facing away from you.

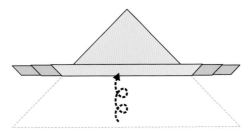

2 Starting from the folded edge nearest to you, roll upwards to the halfway point to form a triangle with two long tails.

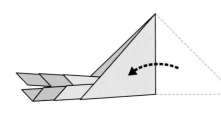

3 Fold the napkin in half from side to side.

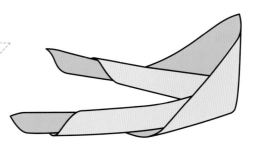

4 Stand the napkin up, pulling the two rolls apart to stabilize it.

EASE	NAPKIN SIZE	SUITABLE MATERIALS	NAPKIN DESIGN	STARCHED
Easy	Small – Medium	Linen – Cotton – Synthetics	Plain	Yes

Collared Bud

Although there are a number of steps to this fold it is not as complicated as it might first seem, especially if paper or starched napkins are used and a little care is taken to make sure the end design is symmetrical. It is perfect for an informal setting, using small napkins with a dainty or colourful design.

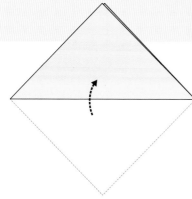

1 Place the napkin reverse side up, one corner towards you, and fold in half from bottom to top to form a triangle with the fold nearest to you.

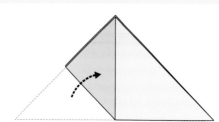

2 Fold the left-hand corner upwards to meet the tip of the triangle so that the bottom edge falls along the centre line.

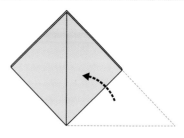

3 Fold the right-hand corner upwards in the same way, with the two bottom edges meeting in the centre.

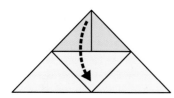

4 Fold in half from bottom to top so that you have a triangle with the fold nearest to you. Turn the napkin over from side to side, keeping the top of the triangle furthest away from you, then fold the top two layers horizontally downwards in half so that the tip just touches the base fold.

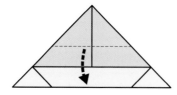

5 Fold the same pieces horizontally in half again, creating a border along the bottom edge.

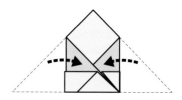

6 Turn the napkin over, then fold the right-hand and left-hand corners over by about a third towards the middle to maintain the symmetry, tucking one side into the folds of the other side to secure it.

7 Stand the napkin upright, arranging the two tall loose triangular flaps to arch over to the sides.

EASE	NAPKIN SIZE	SUITABLE MATERIALS	NAPKIN DESIGN	STARCHED
Intermediate	Small – Medium	Linen – Cotton – Paper	Plain – Patterned	Yes

Lady Windermere's Fan

A traditional fold, this is often found in restaurants and at banquets. The evenness of the pleats is more important than the width, bearing in mind that the wider the pleat, the less formal the result will be. Small paper napkins can be used for large informal gatherings, dotted about the table.

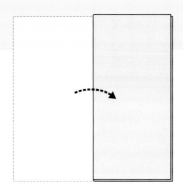

1 Place the napkin reverse side up and fold in half vertically from left to right to form a tall rectangle.

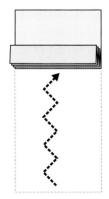

2 Starting at the short end nearest to you, make equal-sized concertina pleats up the napkin, stopping about three-quarters of the way up. If possible use an iron to press the pleats firmly before continuing to the next step.

3 Turn the napkin over, rotate it so that the pleats are underneath on the left-hand side then fold the napkin in half from top to bottom. The pleats will now be on the outside on the left.

4 Fold the bottom right-hand corners upwards, tucking them diagonally under the pleats so that the flat piece of napkin is folded in half to make a triangle.

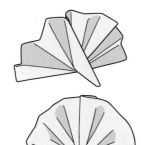

5 Finally, stand the napkin upright so that the triangular piece sits on the surface to steady the pleats, which will fall open to create the fan.

EASE	NAPKIN SIZE	SUITABLE MATERIALS	NAPKIN DESIGN	STARCHED
Easy	Any	Linen – Cotton – Paper	Plain – Bordered	Yes

Oriental Bud

This fold looks particularly appealing when placed in a small bowl – ideal when you are serving a first course such as noodle soup or pasta. It has a modern feel to it, so save it for more informal occasions.

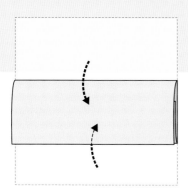

1 Place the napkin reverse side up, then fold the bottom edge upwards to lie along the centre line. Fold the top edge downwards so that it lines up with the bottom edge to form a wide rectangle.

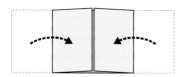

2 Fold the right-hand and left-hand sides to meet along the central vertical line.

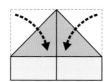

3 Fold the left-hand and right-hand top corners downwards at an angle so that they meet in the middle and the top edges lie along the central vertical line.

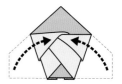

4 Turn the napkin over from side to side. Fold the left and right sides over to the centre by about a third, tucking one side into the other side's folds to secure, making sure you keep the symmetry of the top point.

5 Turn the napkin over vertically and stand it upright.

EASE	NAPKIN SIZE	SUITABLE MATERIALS	NAPKIN DESIGN	STARCHED
Intermediate	Medium – Large	Linen – Cotton – Synthetics	Plain – Patterned	Optional

Guard of Honour

You will need a little patience to achieve this fold. A hot iron, a few needlework pins or a heavy book may prove helpful to keep the folds in place. Although the fold can be done with small napkins, the larger the napkin used, the taller and more impressive the guard of honour's 'sword' will be. Make sure you starch the napkins thoroughly.

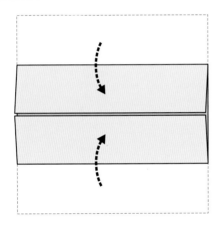

1 Place the napkin reverse side up, then fold the bottom and top edges so that they meet on the centre line, creating a wide rectangle.

2 Holding the edges down in the centre, fold the four loose corners of the napkin backwards on the diagonal, creating a flat shape that looks a bit like a wide, rectangular windmill. If possible, iron all the creases at this step.

3 Starting at the right-hand vertical edge, roll the napkin quite tightly until you get to the centre. Placing a heavy book on the left-hand side while you roll may make it easier to keep the napkin in shape.

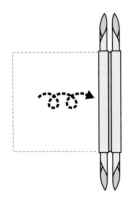

4 Repeat on the left-hand side so that the two rolls meet in the centre. Holding the rolls down firmly, very gently pull each of the centres of the rolls outwards so they lengthen a bit.

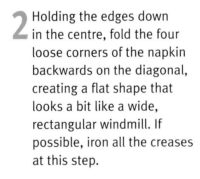
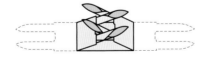

5 Rotate the napkin so that the rolls are horizontal to you, then fold the left-hand and right-hand sides over by a third each so that the rolls interleave with each other.

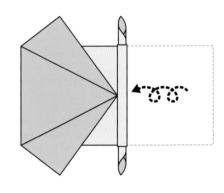

6 Placing cutlery underneath the crossovers may help to stabilize the fold once it is put in place on the table.

EASE	NAPKIN SIZE	SUITABLE MATERIALS	NAPKIN DESIGN	STARCHED
Difficult	Any	Linen – Cotton – Paper	Plain	Yes

CHAPTER 4

Napkins with objects

These folds take napkin folding to yet another level as they all use extra objects as an intrinsic part of the end design. You will need to use your imagination even more when creating many of these folds, especially when it comes to folds which use napkin rings, such as the Posy, as care needs to be taken when matching rings with the napkins.

Choosing natural wood, raffia-type or metal rings will limit the chance of making a mistake in pairing ring with napkin. Alternatively, colour-coordinated ribbon can be substituted for solid napkin rings in many cases. It is also possible to find napkin sets which include rings made from the napkin fabric or a coordinated fabric, so when you are buying new napkins it is worth looking out for these.

Using folds which are placed in glasses not only saves table-top space but also adds height to the setting. One of the easiest folds you can ever learn falls within this group, namely the Simple Wine Glass fold. It is possibly the most versatile of folds, since many types of napkin can be used for both formal and informal occasions.

At the other end of the scale, the Goblet Candle Fan is a lesson in patience and dexterity, not to be attempted if of feeble heart or when in a rush. However, once mastered, it is a very satisfying achievement.

Gathered Fan

This is an informal fold suitable for soft, thin fabrics such as organza and for a matching fabric napkin ring. There is no need to be too precise about the pleats, which can be as large or as small as you like – the larger they are, the softer the look.

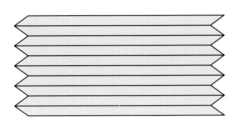

1 Lay the napkin front side up and make horizontal pleats all the way up.

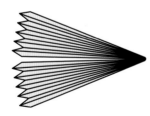

2 Press along the folds, then, holding the pleats together, fold in half from right to left.

3 Take a napkin ring and push the folded edge of the napkin through the ring, just far enough to hold the pleats together. Alternatively, tie the pleats with a decorative ribbon.

4 Turn the napkin so the open ends are facing away from you and fan it out.

EASE	NAPKIN SIZE	SUITABLE MATERIALS	NAPKIN DESIGN	STARCHED
Easy	Small – Medium	Any	Plain – Patterned	Optional

Wine Glass Fan

An informal fold, this is suitable for soft, thin fabrics and a matching fabric napkin ring. It is not necessary to be very exact about the pleats, which can be as large or as small as you care to make them; the wider the pleats, the softer the effect.

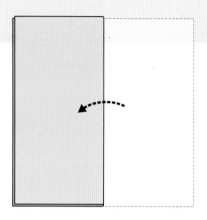

1 Place the napkin reverse side up then fold it in half vertically from right to left.

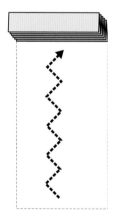

2 Starting from the short edge nearest to you, make pleats all the way up the napkin, keeping them as even as possible.

3 Place the pleated napkin horizontally in front of you with the open ends facing to the left. Fold over the right-hand side about a quarter of the way across and place into a glass, folded side first.

4 Open out the pleats to an attractive fan shape.

EASE	NAPKIN SIZE	SUITABLE MATERIALS	NAPKIN DESIGN	STARCHED
Easy	Medium	Any	Plain – Bordered	Optional

Posy

One of the easiest folds you will ever come across, the Posy is ideal for informal settings. Smaller napkins with colourful prints or laced or scalloped edges work best. Make sure you have the napkin rings ready.

1 Place the napkin right side up.

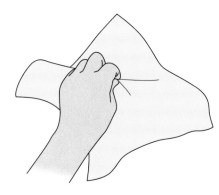

2 Pick up the napkin by holding the centre between two fingers and lifting it vertically, allowing the edges and corners to drape down.

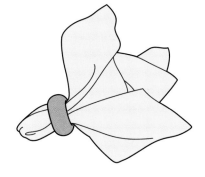

3 Push the centre part of the napkin which you are holding through a napkin ring about halfway through and arrange the open ends into informal folds.

EASE	NAPKIN SIZE	SUITABLE MATERIALS	NAPKIN DESIGN	STARCHED
Easy	Small – Medium	Any	Patterned – Lace-edged – Scallop-edged	Optional

Goblet Candle Fan

This fold requires patience and dexterity. Having a hot iron, a few needlework pins or a heavy book may prove very helpful to keep the folds in place. Although it can be done with small napkins, the larger the napkin used, the taller the 'candles'. Give some thought to the glasses or goblets being used to ensure that the finished look is well-balanced.

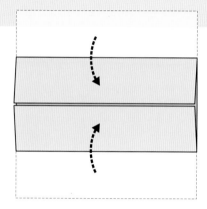

1 Place the napkin reverse side up in a square then fold the top and bottom edges so that they meet on the centre line, creating a wide rectangle.

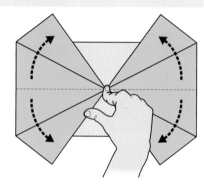

2 Holding the edges down in the centre, fold the four loose corners which you just folded to the centre line backwards on the diagonal. This will create a flat shape that looks a bit like a wide, rectangular windmill. If possible, iron all the creases well.

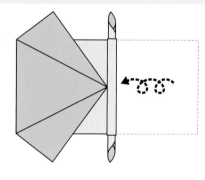

3 Starting at the right-hand vertical edge, roll the right-hand side of the napkin quite tightly, until you get to the centre. Placing a heavy book on the left-hand side while you roll may make it easier to keep the napkin in shape.

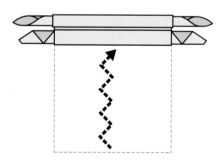

4 Starting at the left-hand vertical edge, pleat the left-hand side, stopping when the pleats meet the rolled part in the centre. Rotate the napkin so the roll and pleats are lying horizontally then, holding the rolls down firmly, very gently pull each of the centres of the rolls outwards so they lengthen a bit.

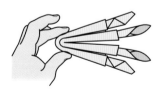

5 Fold the napkin in half, bringing the two ends of the rolled portion together.

6 Place the napkin in a goblet or wine glass folded end first, then arrange the fan pleats and 'candles', spacing them equally in an attractive way.

EASE	NAPKIN SIZE	SUITABLE MATERIALS	NAPKIN DESIGN	STARCHED
Difficult	Medium – Large	Linen – Cotton – Paper	Plain	Yes

Tongs

A very easy fold which is quick to achieve, this works well using most fabrics and paper napkins of all sizes. Use it for informal settings.

1 Place the napkin reverse side up, one corner pointing towards you. Fold almost in half from bottom to top, leaving a narrow border along the top two edges of the resulting triangle.

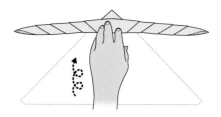

2 Turn the napkin over from side to side then, starting from the long folded edge, roll the napkin upwards quite tightly until you get to the end.

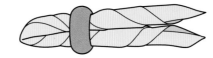

3 Fold the roll in half by bringing the right-hand and left-hand points together, then slip both halves through a napkin ring.

EASE	NAPKIN SIZE	SUITABLE MATERIALS	NAPKIN DESIGN	STARCHED
Easy	Any	Any	Any	Optional

Gifted

Strictly speaking, there isn't any folding involved here at all. The most difficult thing you will have to do is place the object in the centre of the napkin. This fold works with any shape and size of gift – just choose small or large napkins as appropriate. You can even use it to enclose a bread roll. Ribbon or fancy elastic bands can be substituted for napkin rings.

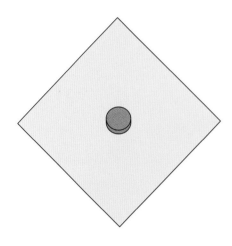

1 Place the napkin reverse side up and place the gift in the centre.

2 Pick up all four corners of the napkin and slip a napkin ring over the ends, pulling the ring down until it just touches the gift.

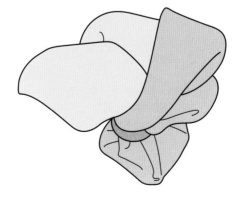

3 Arrange the ends of the napkin in an attractive way: if the fabric is soft and unstarched, allow the ends to fall naturally.

EASE	NAPKIN SIZE	SUITABLE MATERIALS	NAPKIN DESIGN	STARCHED
Intermediate	Medium – Large	Linen – Cotton – Paper	Plain – Bordered	Yes

Goblet Fleur de Lys

As this fold works well with softer fabrics, there is no need to starch the napkin. However, ironing the pleats in place will help the fold to retain its shape once it has been placed in a glass.

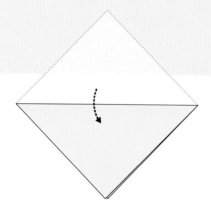

1 Lay the napkin reverse side up, one corner towards you. If you are using a napkin with a corner motif or pattern, place the motif corner at the top. Fold in half from top to bottom to form a triangle with the open ends pointing towards you.

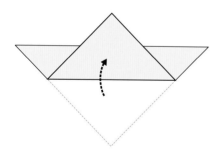

2 Fold the bottom points up so the tips go over the long folded edge by about 5cm/2in.

3 Pleat the napkin from left to right most of the way along, leaving just the very ends unpleated.

4 Holding the pleats in place, insert the bottom edge into a glass which has a stem, such as a wine glass or goblet, allowing the right-hand and left-hand pointed ends to drape over the edge of the glass.

EASE	NAPKIN SIZE	SUITABLE MATERIALS	NAPKIN DESIGN	STARCHED
Intermediate	Medium – Large	Linen – Cotton – Paper	Plain – Patterned	Optional

Place Card Holder

This fold is designed to hold name place cards and while it works well with fabric napkins, it is even better with paper ones. It transports quite well, too, so all the napkins can be pre-folded and taken to the venue ready to place on the tables. Using starched close-weave napkins, such as cotton or linen, helps the folds to stay in place, as does a good pressing. Avoid thick materials.

1 Place the napkin reverse side up with one corner towards you. Fold in half from top to bottom to form a triangle with the open ends facing you.

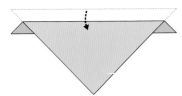

2 Fold the top long edge over to form a border measuring about 2.5cm/1in.

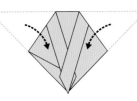

3 Fold the left-hand and right-hand corner points downwards so that they meet in the centre at the bottom point of the triangle.

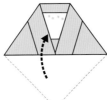

4 Fold the bottom half of the napkin under horizontally, then slip a place card between the top and bottom layers so the name is showing.

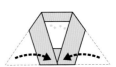

5 Fold the left-hand and right-hand points back and under vertically, so that the front of the fold resembles the neckpiece of a dinner jacket.

EASE	NAPKIN SIZE	SUITABLE MATERIALS	NAPKIN DESIGN	STARCHED
Easy	Small – Medium	Linen – Cotton – Synthetics – Paper	Plain	Optional

Simple Wine Glass Fold

A very easy fold, this is quick to achieve and works well using fine cotton or sheer fabrics. Despite its ease, it can look very formal in the right setting. One of the few folds best made with unstarched napkins, it is a great one to commit to memory as it can be used in most settings and with many types of napkins.

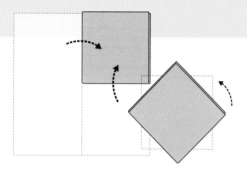

1 Place the napkin reverse side up and fold in half from bottom to top horizontally. Fold in half again vertically to form a square, then rotate the napkin so it forms a diamond shape with the open ends facing away from you.

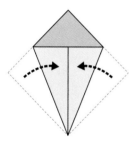

2 Fold the left-hand and right-hand corners over to the centre so that the bottom slanting edges meet along the centre line, creating a cone shape.

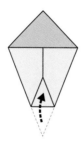

3 Turn the bottom point upwards by about a quarter.

4 Place the napkin in a wine glass, folded edge first.

5 Pull apart the layers which are protruding above the rim of the glass and arrange the folds in an attractive way.

EASE	NAPKIN SIZE	SUITABLE MATERIALS	NAPKIN DESIGN	STARCHED
Easy	Medium – Large	Fine linen – Cotton – Synthetics	Any	No

Menu Minder

As its name suggests, this fold is perfect for holding card menus or even a list of proceedings such as music to be played or items to be auctioned. The only drawback is that it does not transport well, so it is best to make up the folds at the table. Using starched napkins helps the folds to stay in place, as does a good pressing.

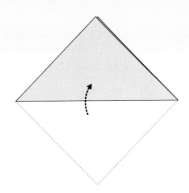

1 Place the napkin reverse side up with one corner towards you. Fold in half from bottom to top to form a triangle with the fold nearest to you.

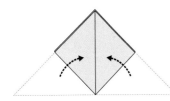

2 Fold the left-hand and right-hand corners upwards to meet the tip of the triangle so that the bottom edges meet along the centre line, forming a diamond shape.

3 Rotate the napkin so that it forms a square made up of two triangles, with the open ends at the top right-hand corner. Fold the top two layers of the top triangle to the left so the point touches the left-hand edge.

4 Fold the same piece in half vertically again to make a wide border at the left-hand side.

5 Fold the top two layers of the remaining triangle downwards so the point touches the bottom edge, then fold in half again horizontally to make a wide border at the bottom edge of the square.

6 Slip the menu underneath the borders then fold the right-hand edge under so that it lines up with the edge of the menu.

EASE	NAPKIN SIZE	SUITABLE MATERIALS	NAPKIN DESIGN	STARCHED
Intermediate	Medium – Large	Linen – Cotton – Paper	Plain – Checked – Striped	Yes

CHAPTER 5

Picnic, buffet and party folds

While a stack of freshly laundered, starched, neatly folded napkins is perfectly welcome on buffet and party tables, putting a little more time into creating an interesting fold will always add more appeal.

Many of the folds in this section have the additional bonus that they double up as carriers of cutlery, making it easy for guests to find what they need in one place, and there are a number of carriers included to suit most occasions. The Tuxedo Pocket is perfect for a formal buffet table, whereas the Simple Silverware Pouch would look at home in the most informal of settings.

Thought should be given as to the food being served with regards to what you include in the pouch-type folds: there is no point including a spoon if everything being served is eaten with a knife and fork.

When choosing a fold which needs to be transported, perhaps for a picnic, think about other items you may wish to include, such as sachets of salt, pepper and mayonnaise, or even individual sachets of wet wipes. An ideal fold for the purpose would be the Al Fresco Parcel – as it is completely enclosed, none of the items can fall out during transport.

Al Fresco Parcel

The Al Fresco fold uses two napkins, making it perfect for outdoor events such as barbecues, when an extra napkin often comes in handy to deal with sticky fingers or spills. Secure enough to stay intact while being transported on a picnic, it is roomy enough to accommodate not just little sachets of salt, pepper, tomato ketchup and so forth but also cutlery.

1 Place the plain napkin reverse side up. Lay the patterned napkin, also reverse side up, on top but slightly lower so that a wide strip of the plain napkin is visible.

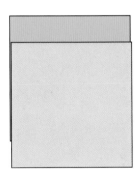

2 Fold the napkins in half vertically, then place the cutlery or other contents vertically in the centre.

3 Fold the right and left sides snugly over the contents.

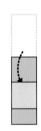

4 Fold the bottom one-third of the napkins upwards.

5 Fold the top downwards and tuck it into the folds of the other end to secure it.

EASE	NAPKIN SIZE	SUITABLE MATERIALS	NAPKIN DESIGN	STARCHED
Easy	Medium	Thicker materials	One plain, one patterned	Optional

Tuxedo Pocket

Ideal for formal buffet or party tables, this fold can be used to hold cutlery neatly. Special care is required to ensure the pleats are of even size and lie perfectly parallel to each other. Using a well-starched napkin and ironing at each stage during folding will make it easier to achieve a sharp finish.

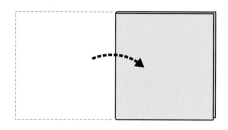

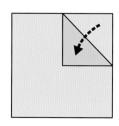

1 Lay the napkin reverse side up then fold in half from bottom to top to form a rectangle with the fold nearest to you.

2 Fold in half from left to right to form a square with all the open ends at the top and right-hand side.

3 Fold the right-hand corner of the top layer diagonally downwards so the point is at the centre of the square.

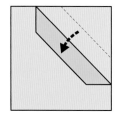

4 Fold it in over again so the newly formed upper flat edge is lying on the centre diagonal line.

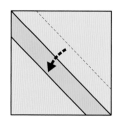

5 Fold it over along the centre diagonal line and press along the folds.

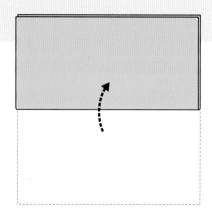

6 Repeat with the second and third layers, individually, slightly overlapping each layer and making sure you keep the pleats parallel and more or less the same depth. Press the folds.

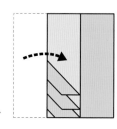

7 Turn the napkin over from side to side then fold the left-hand side over by one third, pressing along the fold.

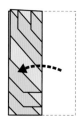

8 Fold the right-hand side over in the same way so it overlaps the left-hand side and tuck it into the fold at the bottom left.

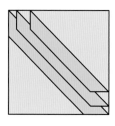

9 Turn the napkin over and iron well before placing cutlery in the top pocket.

EASE	NAPKIN SIZE	SUITABLE MATERIALS	NAPKIN DESIGN	STARCHED
Difficult	Medium	Linen – Cotton – Paper	Plain	Yes

Chevron Pouch

As it can be used to hold cutlery, this fold is great for buffet tables. Use napkins that are absolutely square to ensure that the chevrons line up accurately. Ironing makes for a crisper finish and helps fabric napkins to lie flatter. While plain well-starched napkins are most suitable for more formal occasions, paper napkins are easier to work with, especially if you need a large number.

1 Lay the napkin reverse side up then fold in half from top to bottom so that the open ends are nearest to you.

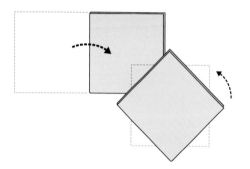

2 Fold in half from side to side to form a square, then rotate the napkin so that it forms a diamond with the open ends facing away from you.

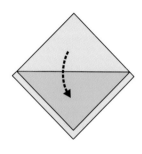

3 Fold down the top layer almost in half, leaving a small border at the bottom two edges. Make sure the borders and edges are even and press down firmly along the fold.

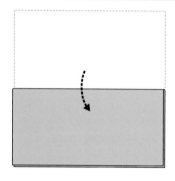

4 Fold down the second and third layers in the same way, once again leaving small borders between the layers and making sure the borders and edges are all even and parallel with each other. Press firmly along all creases.

5 Turn the napkin over from side to side so that it still forms a diamond shape and the layers which have been folded down are underneath and pointing towards you.

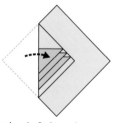

6 Fold the left-hand corner towards the centre by one-third.

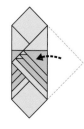

7 Fold the right-hand corner towards the centre in the same way so that it overlaps, then tuck it into one of the flaps. Check for symmetry and press the folds down well. Using an iron may help the napkin to lie flatter.

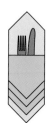

8 Turn the napkin over and place silverware into the pouch

EASE	NAPKIN SIZE	SUITABLE MATERIALS	NAPKIN DESIGN	STARCHED
Intermediate	Medium	Linen – Cotton – Paper	Plain – Bordered	Optional

Double Border Pouch

This fold is ideal for use on buffet or party tables as the cutlery can be placed inside the pouch so that diners can pick up everything they need in one tidy package. It also works well with rectangular napkins.

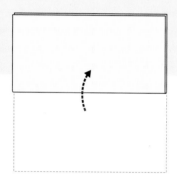

1 Place the napkin right side up then fold in half from bottom to top so the fold is nearest to you. If you are using a striped napkin, make sure the stripes are running vertically.

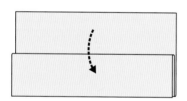

2 Fold the top layer in half downwards.

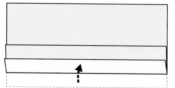

3 Fold all the layers nearest to you in half upwards, creating two borders of equal depth, then press along the creases firmly.

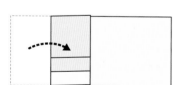

4 Turn the napkin over from side to side so the multi layers are nearest to you, then fold the left-hand side over so the edge lies along the centre line.

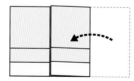

5 Fold the right-hand side over in the same way so that the edges meet in the centre.

6 Fold the napkin in half vertically, tucking one half into the bottom fold of the other half to secure. Turn the napkin over before placing cutlery in the top pouch.

EASE	NAPKIN SIZE	SUITABLE MATERIALS	NAPKIN DESIGN	STARCHED
Easy	Medium	Linen – Cotton – Synthetics	Plain – Striped	Optional

Double-Cuffed Roll

This is an easy fold that doesn't take up much space on buffet tables when the napkins are stacked. Soft or open-weave napkins work well, as do rectangular ones. Use unstarched napkins for a softer effect.

1 Place the napkin reverse side up and fold in half from bottom to top so the fold is nearest to you.

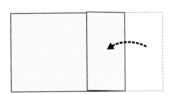

2 Fold the right-hand side to the left so that the edge lies on the centre vertical line.

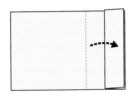

3 Fold the same piece in half back on itself, creating a narrow vertical strip.

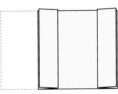

4 Repeat Steps 2 and 3 with the left-hand side.

5 Turn the napkin over from side to side so that the open edges are furthest away from you.

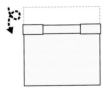

6 Starting at the top open ends, roll the napkin downwards quite tightly, making sure you keep the side edges even.

7 Lay the roll with the seam underneath so that it does not unroll.

EASE	NAPKIN SIZE	SUITABLE MATERIALS	NAPKIN DESIGN	STARCHED
Easy	Small – Medium	Linen – Cotton – Paper	Plain – Bordered	Optional

Nightlight

Suitable for both starched, unstarched, crisp and soft fabrics, this fold creates a very small design – ideal when tabletop space is at a premium, such as at buffet or party tables. A little care is required to get the roll even.

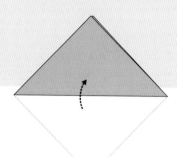

1 Place the napkin reverse side up with one corner towards you. Fold in half from bottom to top to create a triangle with the open ends furthest away from you.

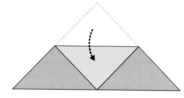

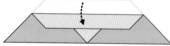  

2 Fold the top point of the triangle downwards so that the tip touches the bottom folded edge.

3 Depending on the size of the napkin, fold the top 2.5–5cm/1–2in over. Continue folding in the same way until the last fold meets the long bottom edge, leaving you with a narrow strip. You may need to adjust this a few times before you get the exact depth.

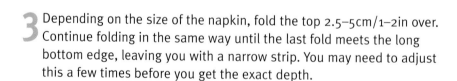

6 Once you get near to the end, fold the last bit upwards to form a little tail, then tuck it into one of the base folds to secure it.

4 Turn the left-hand end of the strip up vertically; this will represent the flame.

5 Beginning at that end and holding the 'flame' in place, start rolling the strip quite tightly, keeping the bottom edges as even as possible.

7 Stand the nightlight up and adjust the protruding end so that it looks like a flame.

EASE	NAPKIN SIZE	SUITABLE MATERIALS	NAPKIN DESIGN	STARCHED
Intermediate	Any	Any	Plain – Self-patterned	Yes

Picnic Roll

As this very simple fold does not take up much room and is suitable to be transported, it is perfect for picnics, buffets or any other occasion where you need to keep cutlery and napkins together neatly. The napkins can be stacked on top of each other to save more space.

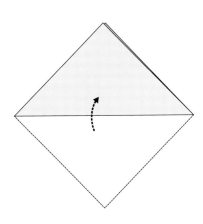

1 Place the napkin reverse side up with one corner towards you. Fold in half from bottom to top, forming a triangle with the fold nearest to you.

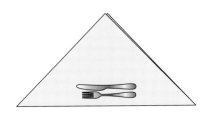

2 Place the cutlery horizontally in the centre, near to the bottom fold.

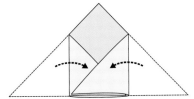

3 Fold the right-hand and left-hand sides over the cutlery. They should overlap.

4 Starting from the bottom, tightly roll the napkin upwards over the cutlery.

EASE	NAPKIN SIZE	SUITABLE MATERIALS	NAPKIN DESIGN	STARCHED
Intermediate	Medium – Large	Linen – Cotton – Paper	Plain – Striped	Yes

Ring Roll

An excellent choice for informal occasions, this simple fold is an easy way to keep sets of cutlery together and is particularly useful for picnics, buffets or party tables.

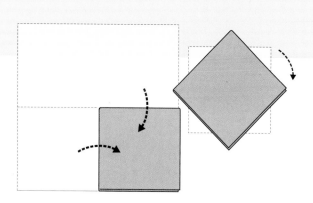

1 Lay the napkin reverse side up and fold in half from top to bottom so that the open ends are nearest to you.

2 Fold in half vertically to form a square. Rotate it to form a diamond then place cutlery vertically in the centre.

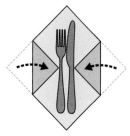

3 Fold the left-hand and right-hand points of the diamond towards the centre so they are nearly touching the cutlery.

4 Fold both sides over to fit snugly around the cutlery then tie with ribbon or slip the roll into a napkin ring.

EASE	NAPKIN SIZE	SUITABLE MATERIALS	NAPKIN DESIGN	STARCHED
Easy	Medium	Any	Plain – Bordered – Patterned	Yes

Simple Silverware Pouch

This fold is quick and easy, making it suitable for large gatherings such as buffets or for casual smaller gatherings for family or friends. Although patterned napkins can be used for informal occasions, this fold looks best with a well-starched plain or bordered napkin.

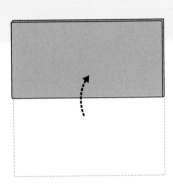

1 Place the napkin reverse side up then fold in half from bottom to top so that the open ends are facing away from you.

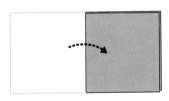

2 Fold the napkin in half from left to right so that the open ends are at the top and right.

3 Fold the top right-hand corner of the top layer in half diagonally and press along the crease.

4 Turn the napkin over from side to side vertically, then fold the left-hand side over by a third.

5 Fold the right-hand side over in the same way, tucking the bottom into the little flap to secure.

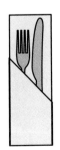

6 Turn the napkin over and place your cutlery in the flap.

EASE	NAPKIN SIZE	SUITABLE MATERIALS	NAPKIN DESIGN	STARCHED
Easy	Medium	Linen – Cotton – Synthetics	Plain – Bordered	Yes

Tri Cable Pouch

This attractive fold is used to hold silverware, making it ideal for formal buffet or party tables. Particular care needs to be taken to ensure that the pleats are even and parallel and the finished napkin is symmetrical.

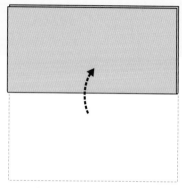

1 Lay the napkin right side up, then fold in half from bottom to top so that the fold is nearest to you.

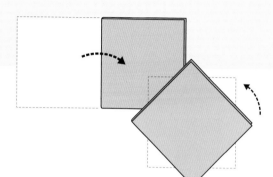

2 Fold in half from side to side to form a square, then turn it to make a diamond with the open ends facing away from you.

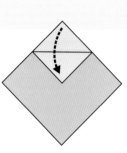

3 Fold the corner of the top layer downwards so the tip is on the centre line.

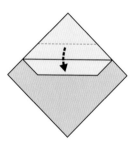

4 Fold it over again so that the top flat edge is lying on the centre line.

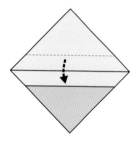

5 Fold it over along the centre line and press firmly along the crease.

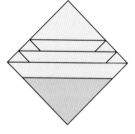

6 Fold the second layer downwards, tucking it behind the first layer and making sure it is the same depth as the first pleat, then repeat with the third layer.

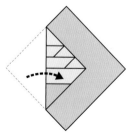

7 Turn the napkin over vertically from side to side, then fold the left-hand side over by one-third and press in place.

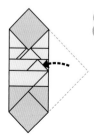

8 Fold the right-hand side over in the same way and tuck into one of the pockets on the left-hand side.

9 Turn the napkin over and place cutlery in the top pocket.

EASE	NAPKIN SIZE	SUITABLE MATERIALS	NAPKIN DESIGN	STARCHED
Intermediate	Medium	Linen – Cotton – Paper	Plain – Striped	Optional

CHAPTER 6

Novelty folds

The folds in this chapter are generally more complex and require more time and dexterity to achieve. However, the end results are worth the effort as many of them can add a real wow factor to table settings, particularly for special occasions and children's events.

The type of napkin to use, with regard to both fabric and pattern, is particularly important in this group as the wrong choice would result in a disappointing finish. If you were to make up the Artichoke fold with a boldly patterned napkin, for example, the beauty would be lost as the clean lines of the many leaves created during the folding process would be obscured by the pattern. Conversely, creating the Moth fold in a plain napkin would not enhance its charm.

If you are very new to napkin folding, pay particular attention to the advice given about the type and size of napkin to be used for each fold in this section. Early investment in a can of spray starch is a must.

Clown's Hat

This is a relatively easy fold which is especially good for children's parties, where brightly coloured napkins go down well. Make sure your napkin is very well starched.

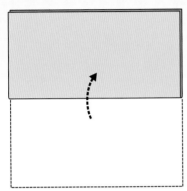

1 Place the napkin reverse side up and fold in half from bottom to top.

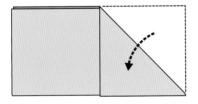

2 Fold the top right-hand corner downwards, with the edges lining up at the bottom.

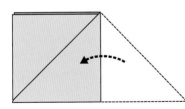

3 Fold the right-hand bottom corner to the left along the centre line so that the edges line up at the bottom.

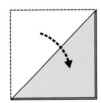

4 Fold the top left-hand corner down to meet the bottom right-hand corner.

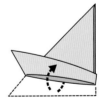

5 Holding the right-hand bottom corners down, place your other hand between the fourth and fifth layers to open up the cone, then carefully turn up a deep hem all the way round. Stand the hat upright.

EASE	NAPKIN SIZE	SUITABLE MATERIALS	NAPKIN DESIGN	STARCHED
Easy	Medium – Large	Linen – Cotton – Paper	Plain – Bordered – Patterned	Yes

Angel Fish

Although this is classed as intermediate, there's only one fold that might prove tricky – the squash fold. However, once you have got the hang of it, the whole thing can be completed quite quickly. Small napkins work best and starched materials or paper napkins create a crisper finish. It is an excellent fold for children's parties.

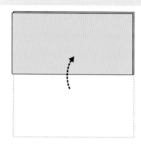

1 Place the napkin reverse side up and fold in half from bottom to top so that the open ends are facing away from you.

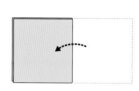

2 Fold the napkin in half from right to left so that the open ends are at the top and left-hand side.

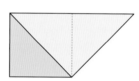

3 With your right hand, take the top left-hand corner of the top layer then, holding the bottom layers down with your left hand, pull the top layer over to the right as far as it will go in a horizontal line. This will automatically pull the bottom left-hand corner upwards to the top centre then push it down to form a triangle, making what is called the squash fold.

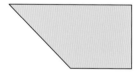

4 Carefully turn the napkin over from side to side.

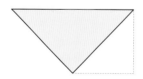

5 With your right hand, take the top right-hand corner of the top layer then, holding the napkin firmly at the bottom mid-point, pull the top layer over to the left as far as it will go in a straight horizontal line. This will pull the bottom right-hand corner upwards to the top centre then push it down to create a triangle.

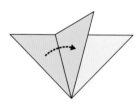

6 Fold the left-hand point of the top two layers over to just past the centre line to make one of the tail fins.

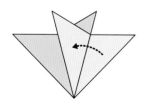

7 Fold the right-hand points of the top two layers over to the left to cover the previous fold, adjusting both folds if necessary to create symmetrical tail fins.

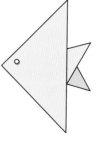

8 Turn the napkin over and use a round sweet or button to represent the fish's eye.

EASE	NAPKIN SIZE	SUITABLE MATERIALS	NAPKIN DESIGN	STARCHED
Intermediate	Small	Any	Any	Yes

Tall Candle

This fold is easy, quick and suitable for all types of occasions from informal to elegant. The choice of napkin is key to the finished article. Choose well-starched large plain napkins for formal affairs or small to medium patterned or colour-coordinated napkins for specific occasions such as Christmas.

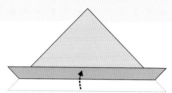

1 Place the napkin reverse side up, one corner towards you. Fold in half from bottom to top to create a triangle.

2 Fold the bottom long edge upwards to a width of 2.5–5cm/ 1–2in, depending on napkin size. Press down well, preferably using an iron, to ensure it stays in place in the following steps.

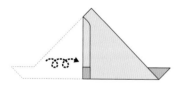

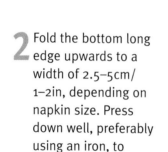

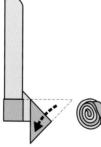

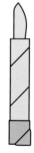

3 Turn the napkin over so that the fold is underneath. Starting at one side, tightly roll the napkin into a slim cylinder, taking particular care to keep the bottom edges even.

4 Once you get near to the end, fold the last bit downwards to form a little tail then tuck it into one of the base folds to secure.

5 At the pointed end, tuck the top little triangular layer under so that the layer underneath forms the flame, then stand upright.

EASE	NAPKIN SIZE	SUITABLE MATERIALS	NAPKIN DESIGN	STARCHED
Easy	Any	Linen – Cotton – Paper	Plain – Patterned – Colour-coordinated	Yes

Whirligig

While this fold is classed as intermediate, there is only one step that is a bit difficult and once it has been mastered, the fold can be quickly finished. It is one of the few complicated folds which can be done with a small napkin, making it an excellent fold for children's parties. Use paper or crisp, starched napkins that easily hold a crease.

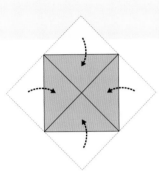

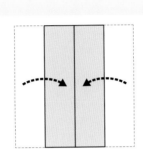

1 Lay the napkin reverse side up, then fold all four corners diagonally so that the points meet in the centre.

2 Fold the right-hand and left-hand sides over to meet in the centre, forming a rectangle.

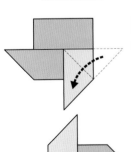

3 Fold the top and bottom edges over so that they meet in the centre, forming a square.

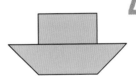

4 Carefully pull out the right-hand and left-hand corners from under the flap nearest to you, holding the napkin down with the other hand, and press along the folds. Using an iron during the next steps will make completion easier.

5 Fold the right-hand point down towards you, which will form two of the blades.

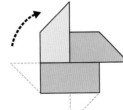

6 Rotate the napkin so that the top straight fold is now nearest to you.

7 Carefully pull out the right-hand and left-hand corners from under the flap nearest to you as you did before, holding the napkin down with the other hand, and press along the folds.

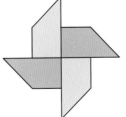

8 Fold the right-hand point down towards you, which will form the last two blades of the whirligig. Press well.

EASE	NAPKIN SIZE	SUITABLE MATERIALS	NAPKIN DESIGN	STARCHED
Intermediate	Small – Medium	Linen – Cotton – Paper	Plain – Gingham – Checked – Spotted – Striped	Yes

Artichoke

This is the fold to use when you want to impress. It consists of many separate folds but most of these are duplicated, so it is not as complicated to achieve as it looks – although you will need some patience and dexterity. For the best effect, use large, plain or self-patterned, starched cotton or cotton-blend napkins.

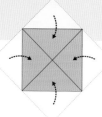

1 Lay the napkin reverse side up then fold all four corners diagonally so they touch in the centre, forming a smaller square.

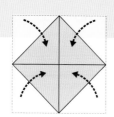

2 Fold the four new corners of the napkin to the centre of the smaller square.

3 Repeat Step 2 to form an even smaller square.

4 Now turn the napkin over then fold all four corners so they touch in the centre as you did before.

5 Turn the napkin back over.

6 Pull up the centre point of each individual square flap and pull backwards just over the outside corners. At this stage, do not pull them out too much.

7 Turn the napkin over again, press firmly with your fingers on the centre of the napkin and pull the flaps under each corner inwards so that they form a cupped edge.

8 Keeping your fingers in place pressing the centre down, reach underneath and gently pull out the flap between each of the last corners created, once again pulling them towards the centre to retain the cupped shape that is formed.

9 Repeat Step 8, pulling the last four single flaps from underneath up and over to form cupped petals.

EASE	NAPKIN SIZE	SUITABLE MATERIALS	NAPKIN DESIGN	STARCHED
Difficult	Large	Fine linen – Cotton – Cotton blends	Plain	Yes

Classic Rose

This fold is ideal for romantic meals or occasions and is compact enough to include on a breakfast tray for Valentine's Day or Mother's Day. It is so easy that even children can make the folds if you want to get them involved in the preparations for setting a special table.

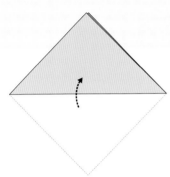

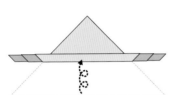

1 Place the napkin reverse side up with one corner towards you. Fold in half from bottom to top to form a triangle with the open ends facing away from you.

2 Starting from the folded edge nearest to you, roll upwards to the halfway point, forming a triangle with two long tails.

3 Turn the napkin over and rotate it so the roll is underneath and the open-ended points of the triangle are facing to the left.

4 Starting from the end nearest to you, roll the napkin tail upwards quite tightly. It will automatically flatten as you roll.

5 When you get to the end of the opposite tail, tuck the last piece into the fold at the top of the roll to secure it.

6 Stand the napkin up, then gently pull apart the two loose flaps at the top and fold them downwards over the sides of the rose.

7 Turn the fold over to reveal a rose plus two leaves.

EASE	NAPKIN SIZE	SUITABLE MATERIALS	NAPKIN DESIGN	STARCHED
Easy	Medium – Large	Linen – Cotton – Synthetics	Plain	Optional

Bunny Rabbit

This is a complicated fold that requires a large napkin and perseverance. It is excellent for children's parties or as a novelty fold for an Easter table. Choose thin cottons or fine linens rather than thicker materials. Stripes, gingham and similar small checks work well, but avoid other patterned napkins. If possible, iron the creases after each step.

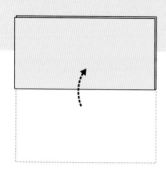

1 Place the napkin reverse side up, then fold in half from bottom to top so that the fold is nearest to you.

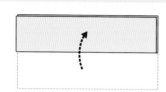

2 Fold the napkin in half from top to bottom again to form a shallow rectangle.

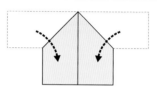

3 Fold the right-hand and left-hand sides at an angle downwards so that the top edges meet on the centre line, forming a point at the top.

4 Fold the bottom left-hand corner upwards so that the left edge is horizontal and its corner touches the centre.

5 Fold the bottom right-hand corner upwards in the same way so that a diamond shape is formed.

6 Fold the right-hand corner diagonally upwards so that the bottom right-hand edge of the original diamond shape is lying vertically along the centre line.

7 Repeat with the left-hand side so that the end shape resembles a kite. Press all the folds thoroughly.

8 Carefully turn the napkin over from side to side to keep the single point at the top.

9 Fold the top point downwards from the widest part.

10 Turn the napkin over.

11 Roll the sides over so that they overlap, then tuck the left-hand side into the little pocket on the right-hand side.

12 Turn the napkin upright, open up its 'face' and adjust the 'ears'.

EASE	NAPKIN SIZE	SUITABLE MATERIALS	NAPKIN DESIGN	STARCHED
Difficult	*Large*	*Linen – Cotton – Paper*	*Plain – Patterned*	*Yes*

Flutterby

This is one of the most complicated folds you will probably ever encounter, requiring patience, dexterity and, despite the detailed instructions, a little imagination. While you can get away with a medium paper napkin, only the largest of fabric napkins will work for this complex fold, preferably made of thin cotton. Starching is a definite help, as is ironing each fold as it is made.

1 Place the napkin right side up and, starting at the bottom, accordion-pleat the bottom half like a fan. The pleats should be as narrow and even as possible to ensure the 'head' of the flutterby is small and compact.

2 Turn the napkin over so that the pleats are lying underneath along the top edge.

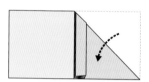

3 Fold the top right-hand corner downwards at a 45-degree angle so that the top edge of the pleats is lying along the centre line and the corner is touching the centre of the bottom edge.

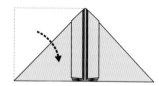

4 Repeat with the left-hand corner so that the top edge of the pleats meets in the centre and the overall shape is a triangle.

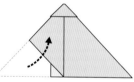

5 Turn the napkin over from side to side vertically, then fold the left-hand bottom corner upwards and tuck it into the little pocket at the top of the triangle.

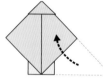

6 Repeat Step 5 with the right-hand corner.

7 Fold the napkin in half from top to bottom.

8 Fold the same piece back on itself so that the little triangular pocket made up of the pleats is just over the top edge.

9 Fold the right-hand corner upwards and over towards the left and tuck it into the top little triangular pocket.

10 Repeat with the left-hand corner.

11 Turn the napkin over and gently spread the pleats a little.

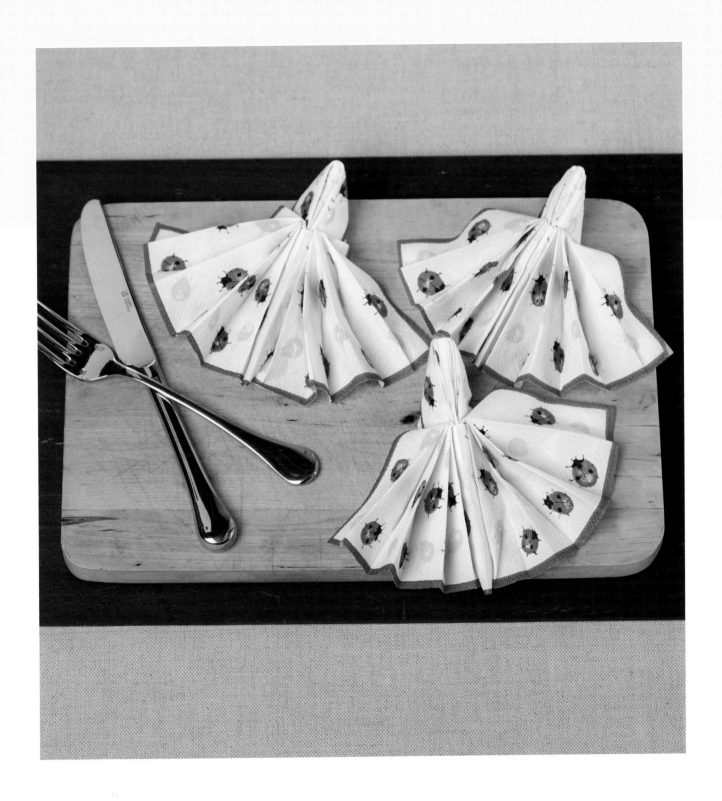

EASE	NAPKIN SIZE	SUITABLE MATERIALS	NAPKIN DESIGN	STARCHED
Difficult	*Large*	*Fine linen – Thin cotton – Paper*	*Plain – Bordered – Small, regular pattern*	*Yes*

Minstrel's Boot

The Minstrel's Boot is a complex fold which requires a little patience to get right. However, it's worth the effort just to see people's reactions – both adult and children alike will be impressed. Choose materials that hold a crease.

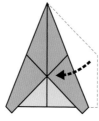

1 Place the napkin reverse side up then fold in half from bottom to top so the fold is nearest to you.

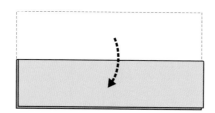

2 Fold the napkin in half again from top to bottom to form a shallow rectangle.

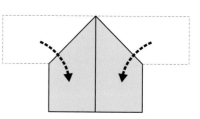

3 Fold the right-hand and left-hand sides at an angle downwards so that the top edges meet on the centre line, forming a point at the top.

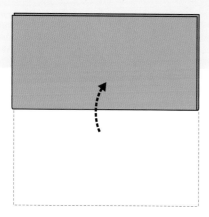

4 Fold the left-hand side down at 45 degrees so that the top slanting edge lies along the centre line.

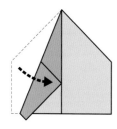

5 Repeat with the right-hand side so that the slanting edge just touches the centre line.

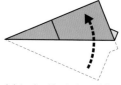

6 Fold in half, right side over the left side. Rotate to the left so the point is facing to the left with the folded part of the top of the 'boot' facing upwards and the two tails on the right.

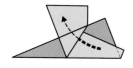

7 Lift up the top tail then fold it under and upwards.

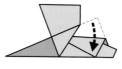

8 Make the lower tail narrower by folding the bottom up and the top down.

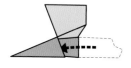

9 Fold the narrowed tail over to the left and tuck it into the pocket which forms the shoe part, pushing it in as far as it will go so that it forms a sturdy heel.

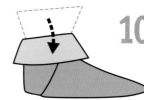

10 Stand the 'boot' up with the toe facing to the right, then fold the top layers over to form the decorative upper part.

EASE	NAPKIN SIZE	SUITABLE MATERIALS	NAPKIN DESIGN	STARCHED
Difficult	Large	Thin linen – Cotton – Paper	Plain	Yes

The Moth

Although many types of napkins can be used for this fold, the best effect is achieved by using well-starched scallop-edged napkins, preferably with a contrast edging. If the napkin has a corner motif, place this at the top right-hand side of the square.

1 Lay the napkin reverse side up, then fold in half from top to bottom so that the open ends are nearest to you.

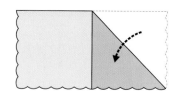

2 Fold the right-hand top corner downwards at a 45-degree angle so that the right edge is lying along the bottom line and the top edge is down the centre.

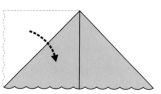

3 Repeat with the left-hand top corner so that the overall shape is a triangle.

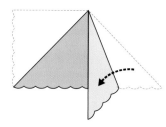

4 Turn the napkin over from side to side, keeping the triangular shape. Fold the right-hand bottom corner downwards to the centre so the right-hand side of the triangle is lying along the vertical centre line.

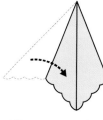

5 Repeat with the left-hand side.

6 Turn the napkin over, then unfold the right-hand and left-hand sides to reveal a triangular pouch on a diamond shape.

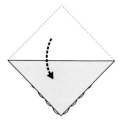

7 Fold in half from top to bottom.

8 Fold the point of the upper layer under and tuck into the triangular pocket to secure.

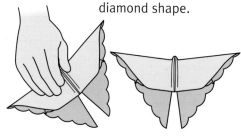

9 Pinch the top folded parts together to form the body, which will pull up the top set of wings and spread out the bottom set. Ironing along each side of the body helps it to keep its shape.

EASE	NAPKIN SIZE	SUITABLE MATERIALS	NAPKIN DESIGN	STARCHED
Intermediate	Small – Medium	Fine linen – Cotton – Thin synthetics	Plain – Patterned	Yes

Folds chart

Name	Type	Ease	Small – up to 30cm/12in	Medium – 32–44cm/13–17in	Large – +45cm/18in	Linen, cotton	Thin materials	Synthetic mixes	Paper	Plain	Patterned	Starch
Summer Bud	Flat	Easy	●	●		●	●	●	●	●	●	●
Clutch Bag	Flat	Easy	●	●	●	●	●	●	●	●	●	●
Tri Pleat	Flat	Easy	●	●		●		●	●	●	●	●
Water Lily	Flat	Intermediate		●	●	●	●	●		●		●
Humetty Cross	Flat	Difficult	●	●	●	●		●		●	●	●
Iced Diamond	Flat	Intermediate	●	●		●		●	●	●		●
Kimono	Flat	Intermediate	●	●	●	●	●	●	●	●		●
Mortar Board	Flat	Intermediate	●	●	●	●	●	●	●		●	●
Palm Leaf	Flat	Easy	●	●		●	●	●	●	●		●
Purity Square	Flat	Intermediate	●	●		●		●	●	●	●	●
Spearhead	Flat	Intermediate	●	●		●		●	●	●	●	●
Spring Roll	Flat	Easy	●	●		●	●	●	●	●		●
Steps	Flat	Intermediate	●	●		●		●	●	●	●	●
The Pyramid	Standing	Easy	●	●		●		●	●	●	●	●
Atrium Lily	Standing	Difficult	●	●	●	●		●		●		●
The Marquee	Standing	Easy	●	●	●	●		●	●	●	●	●
The Crown	Standing	Intermediate	●	●	●	●		●		●	●	●
Waterfall	Standing	Intermediate	●	●	●	●		●	●	●		●
Bird of Paradise	Standing	Difficult		●	●	●		●		●	●	●
Bishop's Mitre	Standing	Intermediate	●	●	●	●		●	●	●	●	●
Cardinal's Hat	Standing	Easy	●	●	●	●		●	●	●		●
Catamaran	Standing	Easy	●	●		●		●	●	●	●	●
Collared Bud	Standing	Intermediate	●	●		●		●	●	●	●	●
Lady Windermere's Fan	Standing	Easy	●	●		●		●	●	●	●	●
Oriental Bud	Standing	Intermediate	●	●		●		●	●	●		●
Guard of Honour	Standing	Difficult	●	●		●		●	●	●		●
Gathered Fan	Objects	Easy	●	●		●	●	●	●	●	●	●
Wine Glass Fan	Objects	Easy		●		●	●	●	●	●	●	●

Key: Optional ▢